INSTANT CHRISTMAS PAGEANT:
Live From Bethlehem

by
Bob Latchaw
and
Cindy Hansen

Loveland, Colorado

**Instant Christmas Pageant:
Live From Bethlehem**

Copyright © 1992 Group Publishing

All rights reserved. No part of this book may be reproduced in any manner whatsoever without written permission from the publisher, except where noted in the manuscript and in the case of brief quotations embodied in critical articles and reviews. For information write Permissions, Group Publishing, Inc., Dept. BK, Box 481, Loveland, CO 80539.

Credits
Edited by Stephen Parolini
Designed by Liz Howe and Diane Whisner
Cover illustration by Dennis Jones
Cover design by Jean Bruns
Interior illustrations by Rand Kruback

ISBN 1-55945-095-9
13 12 11 10 9 8 7 6 5 4   04 03 02 01 00 99 98
Printed in the United States of America.

Live From Bethlehem
Contents

How to Use This Pageant 4

Assigning the Roles 7

Creating the Costumes 8

Preparing the Props 11

Publicizing the Pageant 21

Singing With the Congregation 22

Setting the Stage 23

Live From Bethlehem: The Script 24

Christmas Carol Lyrics 45

How to Use This *Pageant*

Congratulations! Most of the hard work in preparing your children's Christmas pageant is already done! You hold the result of that work in your hands right now—*Live From Bethlehem*, an *Instant Christmas Pageant*.

Live From Bethlehem provides you with a complete Christmas program on cassette. All the spoken dialogue, sound effects and music are prerecorded. You even get songs for the whole congregation to sing along with the children.

This *Instant Christmas Pageant* is flexible. Your kids can perform it for:

- a Sunday morning service,
- an afternoon or evening children's program,
- a family night program,
- a special Sunday school program,
- a nursing home program and more!

And it can be performed by children from age four through 84.

Even teenagers and senior citizens will enjoy putting on this pageant! Or you can have a puppet group perform the pageant.

Live From Bethlehem is easy to prepare for, too. Just follow these simple steps:

1. Read the rest of this book, and listen to the cassette.
2. Photocopy the clip art on page 21 to decorate fliers, bulletins and poster publicizing the pageant.
3. Determine how you'll adjust the number of roles in the play to match the number of children who'll be in your program. You'll find a few ideas on how to add or subtract to the roles on page 7.
4. Have kids help you collect and create costumes and props. Many props can be collected from kids' homes. And the rest can be created using the photocopiable patterns beginning on page 11.
5. Play the cassette for your children. Then assign parts to children.
6. Practice the play with your children. Here's the fun part—kids don't need to memorize their lines! Don't have them lip-sync the parts, either. Instead, direct kids to follow the action and movement instructions in the script. After one or two times through, kids will know how to pantomime all the actions needed! Or have kids come up with their own actions.
7. Perform the play. During the play, invite the congregation's participation in singing along with the Christmas carols.

It's that simple!

Here are a few tips to help you get the most of *Live From Bethlehem:*

● Practice the actions and movements a few times so kids feel comfortable with their roles before a performance.

● Because each sanctuary setup is different, you may want to pause the cassette during the pageant, allowing time for kids to move across the stage.

● Have a child or adult volunteer introduce the pageant before hitting the "play" button on your cassette player. This is a good time to let the congregation know they'll be singing along during the pageant.

● Use teenagers, adults or senior citizens to supplement roles if you don't have a large enough group of children.

● Increase the length of your program by having children read aloud sections of Luke's account of Jesus' birth before, during or after the play.

● The entire program is on side A of the cassette for your convenience. The other side of the cassette is blank.

● Read and discuss Luke 2:1-20 with your children as you prepare for the program. Use the costume-creation and rehearsal times as mini-Bible studies.

ASSIGNING THE *Roles*

One of the best features of *Live From Bethlehem* is that almost any role can be played by any child in your church. Since the spoken parts are prerecorded and kids don't need to memorize lines, young children can become the main characters as easily as older children. A few roles, such as Esther and Jacob, are probably best suited to older children, however, since the suggested actions and facial expressions are more involved.

Each role in *Live From Bethlehem* is listed in the Creating the Costumes section.

If you have fewer than 21 children, combine roles. For example, one person could play Angela The Innkeeper and a shepherd simply by changing the color of the towel over her head. Another person could play one of the Jones' children and a commercial announcer by putting on a different bathrobe for the commercial. Or teenagers and adults can help out by playing such roles as the commercial announcers or Mary and Joseph.

If you have more than 21 children, increase the number of children in the Jones family, the number of commercial announcers, the number of travelers or the number of shepherds. Or form a separate children's choir to lead the congregation in singing the hymns.

CREATING THE
Costumes

Most characters can use the standard "biblical bathrobe" for the main part of their costume. Other costume elements and props are suggested in this section for each character. Using the photocopiable patterns beginning on page 11, you can create such props as the Magi's crown, Shekel's visor, The Star of Bethlehem, press cards, and more.

ELIZABETH—*Middle-aged news reporter. A polished, professional anchor-woman.*

　　Suggested costume accessories: Towel turban and chain necklace.

ZACH—*Young, enthusiastic travel correspondent.*

　　Suggested costume accessories: Walking stick, press card attached to his costume (see page 17 for press card pattern.)

ESTHER AND DAVE JONES—*Middle-aged couple heading to Bethlehem for the census.*

　　Suggested costume accessories: Camera for Dave, diaper bag for Esther.

THE JONES KIDS—*Dave and Esther's energetic children. These kids can come in all shapes, sizes and ages. They're excited about the trip to Bethlehem.*

Suggested costume accessories: Baseball caps, sneakers and stuffed animals.

TRAVELERS—*People who walk by the interview scene and wave at the camera.*

Suggested costume accessories: Suitcases.

COMMERCIAL ANNOUNCERS—*One announcer for the Kwik Kleen Camel Cleaner commercial; one or more announcers for the Census commercial and one announcer for the Net Menders commercial.*

Suggested costume accessories: For the Census commercial, announcers could each carry a clipboard. For the Net Menders commercial, the announcer could hold a net with a big hole in it.

SHEKEL SMITH—*Near-retirement, business reporter.*

Suggested costume accessories: An accountant's visor (See page 15 for a visor pattern), white shirt and pencil behind his ear.

ANGELA THE INNKEEPER—*Older woman. She's used to the hustle and bustle of the census.*

Suggested costume accessories: Apron and broom.

OBADIAH—*Staff "weatherologist." Adds his own personality to the weather reports.*

Suggested costume accessories: Necktie and open umbrella.

JACOB—*Young, energetic field reporter.*

Suggested costume accessories: Beach hat, sunglasses, sun block and a press card attached to his hat. (See page 17 for press card pattern.)

MAGI MIKE, MARK AND MELISSA—*The three kings who visit Jesus.*

Suggested costume accessories: Crowns. (See page 12 for a crown pattern.) Bright-colored robes and gold- or silver-colored belts.

IRENE—*Young, on-the-scene reporter.*

Suggested costume accessories: Fedora hat with press card. (See page 17 for press card pattern.) A winter coat over her bathrobe.

SAM—*A shepherd.*

Suggested costume accessories: Towel turban and shepherd's staff (an old broom handle that looks like a walking stick).

MARY AND JOSEPH—*Traditional Mary and Joseph stand in manger scene during the entire pageant.*

Suggested costume accessories: Robes and other costume elements as depicted in traditional paintings of the manger scene.

THE BETHLEHEM STAR—*The star of Bethlehem.*

Suggested costume accessories: Yellow or orange shirt and pants and cardboard star. (See page 18 for star pattern.)

PREPARING THE
Props

Most of the props you'll use in *Live From Bethlehem* can be created using the patterns on the following pages. In addition to these props, you'll need each character's suggested costume accessories, a card table, microphones, a manger scene, a bottle, a bucket, a flashlight and a doll to be the baby Jesus.

Photocopy the following props and follow the instructions in the provided illustrations to create the props used in the pageant.

MAGI MIKE, MARK AND MELISSA'S CROWNS

TAPE OR STAPLE ON AN EXTRA PIECE OF PAPER TO MAKE YOUR CROWN FIT YOUR HEAD.

Permission to photocopy this handout granted for local church use. Copyright © Group Publishing, Inc., Box 481, Loveland, CO 80539.

KWIK KLEEN KAMEL KLEENER BOTTLE COVER

20 KAMEL TEAM STRENGTH BUCKET COVER

SHEKEL SMITH'S ACCOUNTANT VISOR

"NO VACANCY" SIGN

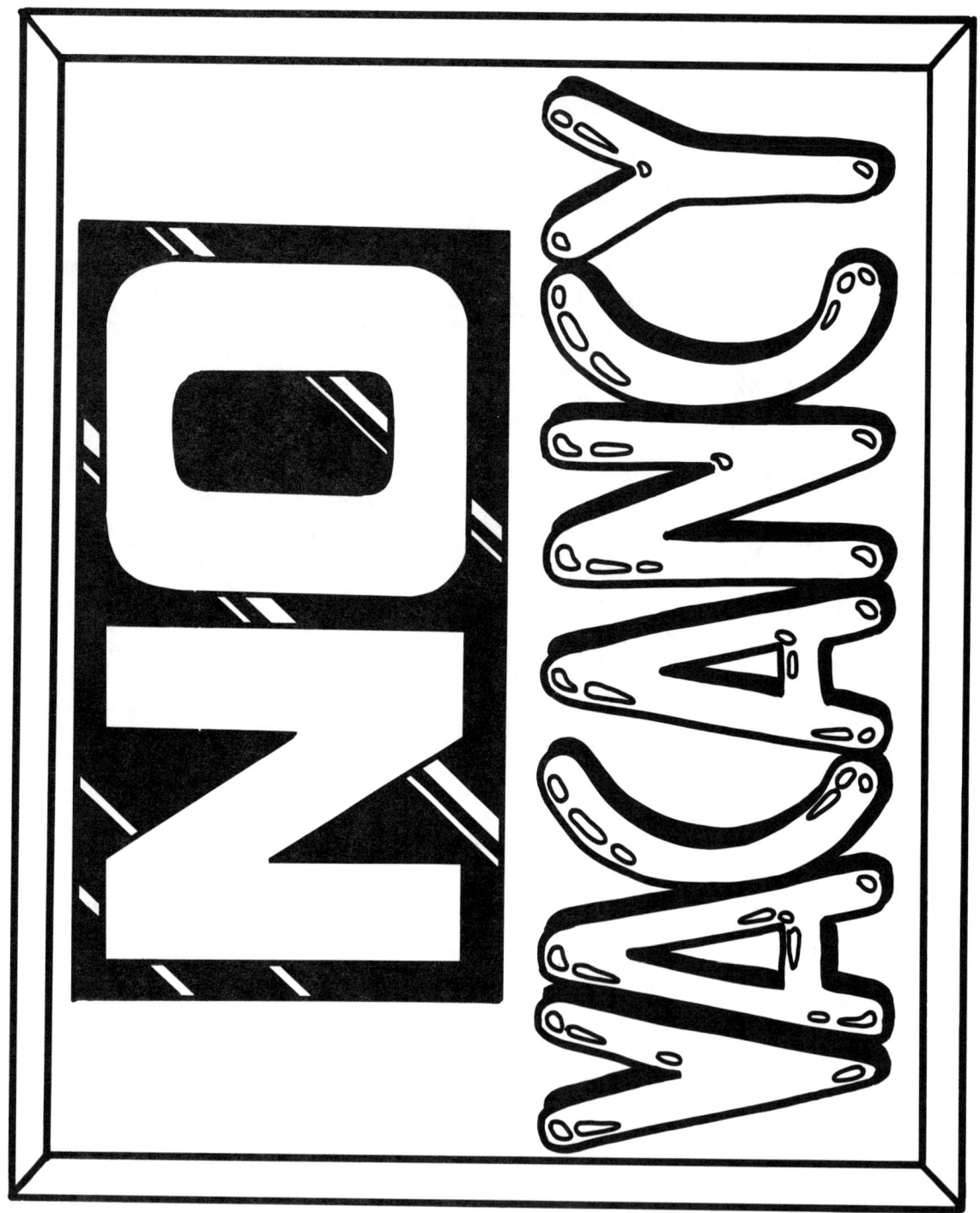

PRESS CARD

17

THE STAR OF BETHLEHEM

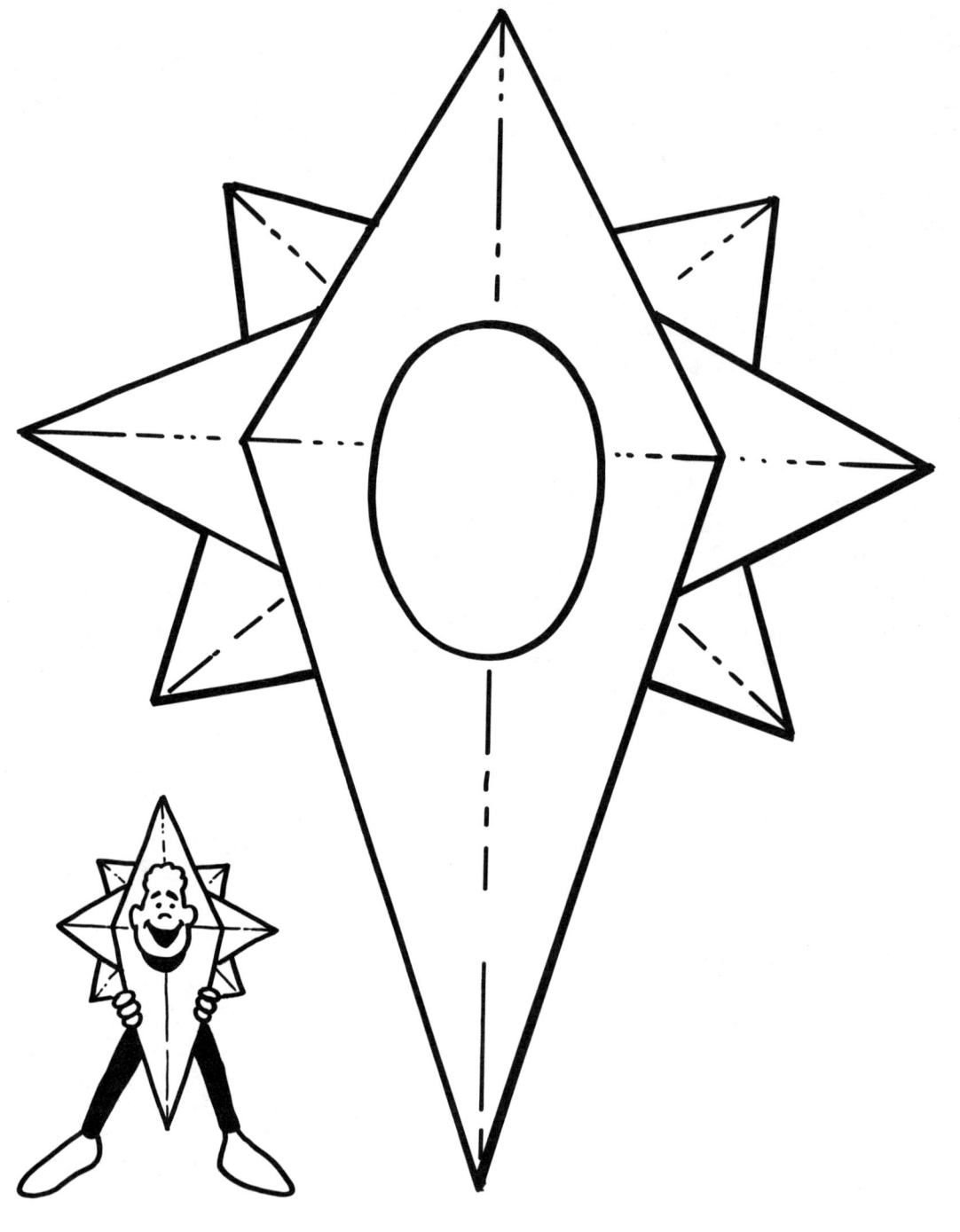

BBS MICROPHONE LOGO

BETHLEHEM BROADCASTING SYSTEM POSTER

Publicizing the *Pageant*

Photocopy the clip art on this page to publicize your children's performance of *Live From Bethlehem*. Use the clip art on fliers, bulletins or posters. Or simply add the appropriate performance information to the half-page flier below to use as a bulletin insert.

Permission to photocopy this handout granted for local church use. Copyright © Group Publishing, Inc., Box 481, Loveland, CO 80539.

 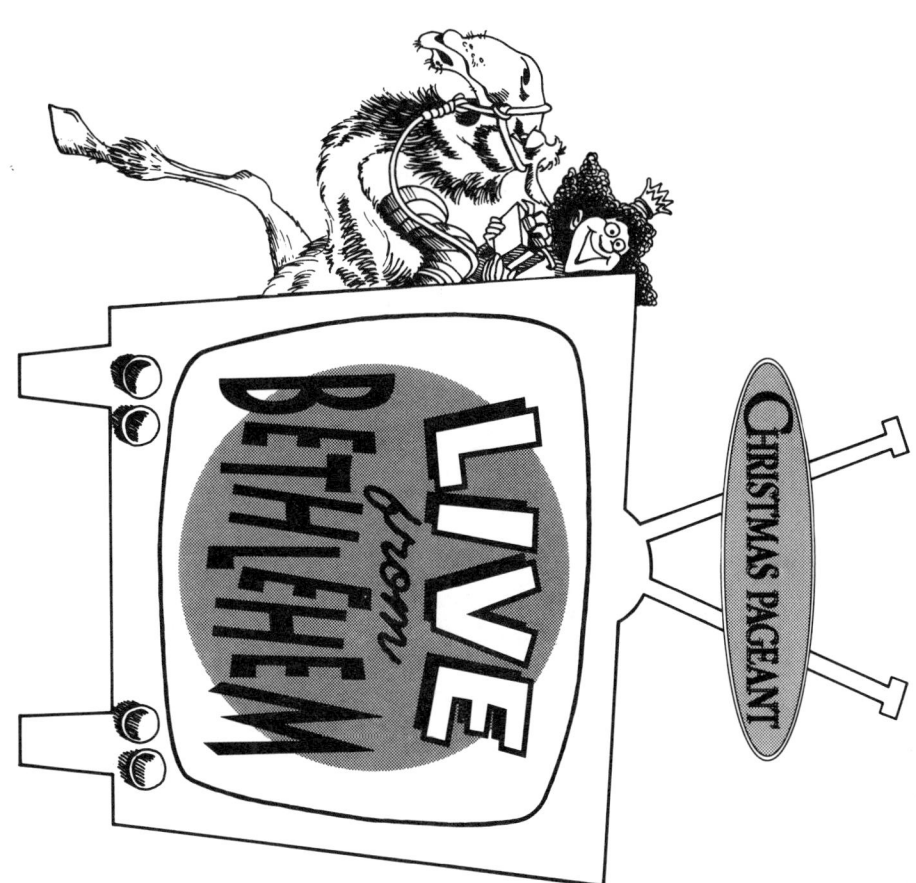

SINGING WITH THE *Congregation*

The songs in *Live From Bethlehem* are familiar Christmas carols. But just in case some congregation members don't know all the words, photocopy the flier on page 45 and pass it out at the beginning of the pageant.

SETTING THE
Stage

Use the following diagram to set your stage. Adjust the location of the props according to the space you have in your church.

Tape the Bethlehem Broadcasting System poster (see page 20) to the front of the card table used as the anchor-person's desk. Attach the BBS microphone logo (see page 19) to a real microphone placed on the anchor-person's desk and a BBS logo to each microphone used by Zach, Jacob and Irene. The microphones are simply props and don't need to be turned on during the pageant.

Most action takes place at center stage. Place the news desk on the opposite side of the stage from the manger scene.

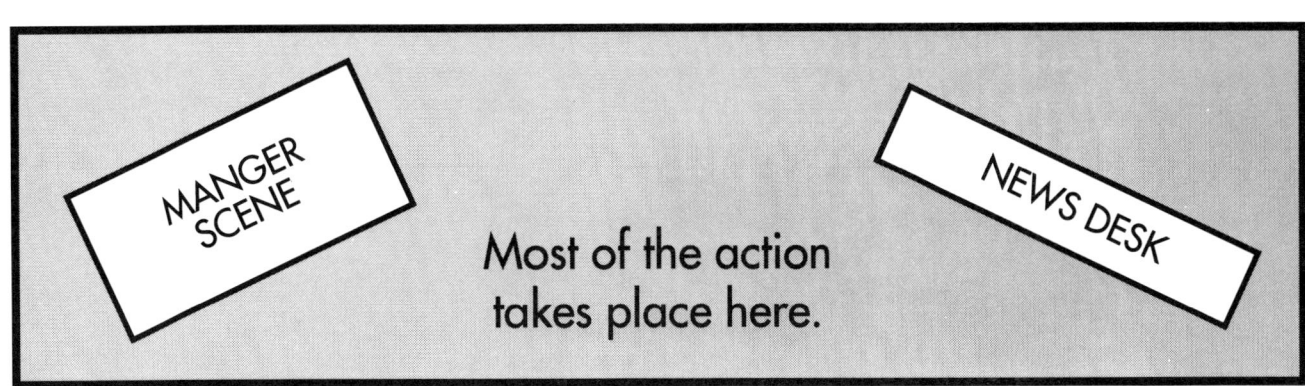

AUDIENCE

Live From Bethlehem
The Script

Use this script to familiarize yourself with the dialogue and actions in *Live From Bethlehem*. Remember, kids don't need to memorize these lines or even lip-sync the words to the tape.

Scattered throughout the script are suggestions to assist you in planning the movement and action for the Christmas pageant. Your kids may think up new ideas and actions — that's great! Incorporate their ideas into the pageant as much as possible.

Have someone introduce the pageant and remind the congregation that they'll be singing along with the carols during the program.

OVERTURE *(Play as audience enters)*

◆ As news theme starts, Elizabeth enters and sits at news desk.

◆ Elizabeth sits at news desk stage left where she remains for the entire play.

◆ Zach enters from stage left and stands center stage for his part.

ELIZABETH: ◆ *Proudly, network-news-anchorstyle*
Good evening, and welcome to the Bethlehem Broadcasting System news. I'm Elizabeth of Jerusalem. Tonight: A special report on the census. The recent decree for a census has caused a flurry of activity in and around Judea. But before the counting can begin, thousands of people must wind their way home to their birthplaces from the far corners of our fair land. Let's go now to a live report just outside Bethlehem. Here is our travel correspondent, Zach, the Samaritan.

◆ The Jones family—Dave, Esther and the children—enter stage left and move slowly to stage right.

ZACH: ◆ *Looking at congregation as though looking into a TV camera*
Thank you, Elizabeth. As you can see behind me, there's a steady stream of travelers heading into town.
   ◆ Zach stops Esther who's leading her children.
   ◆ Dave is bringing up the rear, taking pictures.

Excuse me, ma'am, what's your name?

◆ Esther abruptly stops, her children bump into each other—domino-style.

◆ Dave is oblivious to the action, because he has stopped a few feet earlier to take a picture.

ESTHER: ◆ Looks around for the TV camera
Oh! Hello! Am I on TV?

◆ Waves excitedly

◆ Travelers occasionally wander by behind this scene—waving to the camera, nudging each other and pointing.

◆ Esther's kids join in on the act by waving at the imaginary TV camera.

ZACH: ◆ Holding a microphone at his mouth
Yes, ma'am, may we have your name please?

◆ Zach moves microphone to Esther's mouth.

ESTHER: Esther. E-S-T-H-E-R from the Eastern valley.

◆ Zach moves microphone to his mouth.

ZACH: And, Esther, why are you heading into Bethlehem?

◆ Zach moves microphone to Esther's mouth.

ESTHER: I'm going with my husband. He needs to be counted in the census. Dave, come over here!

◆ Esther grabs her husband, who hasn't noticed the reporter and is still taking pictures.
Dave! Look! We're on TV!

DAVE: ◆ He looks around.
TV? No... Really? Well, bust my seams.
◆ Dave takes a picture of Zach.

ZACH: ◆ Zach looks at Dave patiently, then holds microphone at his own mouth.
Yes, sir. So, you're a native of Bethlehem?
◆ Zach moves microphone to Dave's mouth

DAVE: ◆ Dave puts his thumbs in his armpits and sticks his chest out.
Born and raised here! I'm a tent-maker by trade, as was my father and my father's father and my father's father's...

ZACH: ◆ Zach quickly moves microphone to his own mouth.
We get the picture, thank you.

DAVE: Sorry.

ZACH: Tell us about your trip.

DAVE: ◆ Zach moves microphone to Dave's mouth.
◆ Calming down a bit.

Well, it wasn't too bad. The road's okay. And, ummm, you meet some nice people.

◆ **Zach moves microphone back and forth between Dave and Esther trying to keep up with their dialogue.**

ESTHER: Oh, tell him about the nice young couple we met the first night out, dear.

DAVE: Oh, yeah.
◆ **Scratching head**
Ummm, what were their names? Uh, uh, Joseph and... and... and...

ESTHER: ◆ **Turns toward Dave with her hands on her hips**
Mary!

DAVE: Sorry.

ESTHER: She was the sweetest young thing—and very pregnant!

DAVE: ◆ **Chuckling**
Yeah, they were both really nervous. Obviously their, uh, first child. You know, I remember when Esther and I had our first child. It was a stormy night in s...

ESTHER: ◆ **Jabs Dave with her elbow**
I think he gets the picture.

DAVE: Sorry.

ESTHER: Tell him about the couple.

DAVE: Well, we left them behind that next day. You know, Joseph was kinda keeping a slow pace 'cause of Mary's condition, you, you know.

ZACH: ◆ **Zach moves microphone to his own mouth.**
Yes. Well, it looks like the crowd is thinning out here, Elizabeth. In fact, we're almost the only ones left. The little town of Bethlehem is becoming quite still.
◆ **Turns to audience**
Will you sing with us?

◆ **Cast and congregation sing "O Little Town of Bethlehem."**

ESTHER: Well, we'd better keep moving if we expect to find a room for the night!

DAVE: Sorry.
◆ **Whispering to Zach**
Always worrying for nothin'. You know, I'm sure there are plenty of rooms, if we're not too picky.
◆ **Family waits next to Zach as he wraps up his interview.**

ZACH: Well, that's the story from the road to Bethlehem.

DAVE: Bye. ◆ **Dave waves goodbye.**
Oh, uh, sorry.

ZACH: Back to you, Elizabeth.

ELIZABETH: Thanks, Zach.
◆ **Zach and family exit.**
◆ **Announcer enters from stage left and walks to center stage.**
We'll be right back with more news after this commercial break.

COMMERCIAL ANNOUNCER: Say, are you bothered by the odor your favorite camel gives off after a long day under the sun? Is your stable beginning to draw flies? After a long day on your camel's back, does your spouse say, "Welcome home 'sweaty'" instead of "sweety"? Well, come clean with Kwik Kleen Kamel Kleener. It really does the trick, and it's so easy to use! Simply rub the pleasant smelling lotion on your camel's skin once every hour for three days and before you can say Shadrach, Meshach and Abednego you'll have the sweetest smelling dromedary on the block.

◆ **Sniffs bottle**

And it smells great, too! So remember, look for Kwik Kleen Kamel Kleener in the easy roll-on bottle. And for those stubborn smells, try new 20 Kamel Team Strength in the 5-gallon bucket.

◆ **Announcer holds up bucket, then exits stage left.**

◆ **As news theme plays, Shekel, the reporter, enters from stage left and stands center stage.**

◆ **Angela The Innkeeper enters from stage right and stands closer to the manger.**

ELIZABETH: Continuing our special report, the census has created a tremendous impact on Bethlehem's hotel industry. For more on this story, we go to our business reporter, Shekel.

SHEKEL: ◆ **Shekel holds a microphone at his mouth.**
Did you ever need a room for the night but couldn't find one? Even a cut-rate one that doesn't put a chocolate on your pillow or give you a little coffeepot and a premeasured packet of coffee? Well, be glad you aren't a traveler staying in this town tonight. Due to the census, the inns are full, and there isn't a room to be found.
◆ **Shekel turns and rings doorbell at inn.**
◆ **After doorbell rings, Angela The Innkeeper opens the door and steps outside holding a "No Vacancy" sign.**
Excuse me, but I don't suppose you have any rooms?

◆ **Angela The Innkeeper rolls her eyes as though to say, "Who is this guy?" and points to the "No Vacancy" sign.**

SHEKEL: Oh, yes. I see. What if I told you that I'm a famous reporter for the Bethlehem Broadcasting System?

◆ **Shekel moves microphone to Angela's mouth, then back to his own throughout dialogue between Angela and him.**

ANGELA: There's no room at the inn!!

SHEKEL: Not even a little room?

ANGELA: No. No room.

SHEKEL: How about a closet?

ANGELA: ◆ **Angela puts her hands on her hips.**
Look, buddy, what part of "no" don't you understand?

SHEKEL: Well, ummm...

ANGELA: I'll tell you how bad it is. I had a couple stop in earlier this evening. He looked dog-tired, and she, she was obviously close to having a baby. I had to turn even them away.

SHEKEL: That's awful!

ANGELA: Well, yeah, it didn't make me feel too good, either. I had a family of my own. But, like the sign says, no vacancy. Anyway, the best I could do was to direct them to the stable out back. At least there's a manger filled with hay, I mean, in case the baby's born tonight, ya know.
◆ **Shivers**
Brrr. Is it getting cold out here or what? I think I'll get 'em some more blankets.

◆ **Door creaks as Angela goes inside to get blankets.**

SHEKEL: It's so nice to see a little human kindness in this old world.

◆ **Door creaks. Angela comes outside with several blankets.**

SHEKEL: Well, if you arrive in Bethlehem tonight, it looks like stables are all that's left.
　◆ **Pauses looking thoughtfully**
Imagine sleeping in a manger. Hmmm, away in a manger.
　◆ **Shekel motions to audience.**
Ahh, that reminds me of a song... let's hear it.

◆ **Congregation and cast sing "Away in a Manger."**

SHEKEL: Reporting on the "inns" and outs of the hotel business, I'm your business reporter, Shekel.
　◆ **Shekel exits stage left.**

ELIZABETH: Thank you, Shekel. We'll be back with the weather right after this.
　◆ **Sound effect - news theme**
　◆ **Sound effect - music for commercial**
　◆ **As music plays, commercial announcers enter from stage left and stand center stage.**

COMMERCIAL ANNOUNCERS:
◆ **Singing, while counting members of the audience**
One little, two little, three little people, four little, five little, six little people, seven little, eight little, nine little people, mark ten in our book.
◆ **They continue humming the tune while one announcer steps forward.**

COMMERCIAL ANNOUNCER: The census isn't senseless. It's the LAW!
◆ **Singers exit stage left.**
◆ **News theme begins. Obadiah enters from stage left and stands center stage.**

ELIZABETH: Welcome back to the Bethlehem Broadcasting System News.
◆ **Elizabeth turns to Obadiah.**
Well, how's that family in the stable going to feel before tonight's over, Obe.

OBADIAH: Well, in all my years as a staff weatherologist, I don't think I've ever recommended covering up your people as well as your plants.
◆ **Obadiah laughs, realizes no one else is laughing, then clears throat.**
Ummm. They might be a tad chilly. However, the days will be right pretty. The insects are plentiful and that indicates a wet spring with plenty of thunderstorms. And the camel grass is still green which means

the herds will have plenty of food.

◆ **As music begins, Jacob and The Bethlehem Star enter from stage right and stand between center stage and manger.**

OBADIAH: ◆ **Commercial announcer enters and hands Obadiah a sheet of paper. Obadiah looks at it.**
Oh, this just in. We're getting some reports of an unusually bright star located over the downtown Bethlehem area. As a matter of fact, those who've seen it say it's the brightest star they've ever seen! We have a reporter on location right now. Jacob, can you hear me? Are you there?

◆ **Night sounds, street party and Jamaican music begin. Cast, including Magi, moves into audience.**
◆ **They are dancing and happy.**
◆ **Slowly they all move on stage.**

◆ **Jacob, wearing sunglasses, blocks the rays with his hand.**
◆ **The Bethlehem Star shines a flashlight on Jacob.**
◆ **Jacob holds a microphone at his mouth with his other hand.**

JACOB: I hear you fine, Obadiah. The star is extremely bright. It seems to be shining a beautiful clear beam of starlight down somewhere in Bethlehem.
◆ **The Bethlehem Star points flashlight stage right—the direction for Jacob to go**
The people are getting really excited. Can you hear this crowd behind me? It sounds like they're starting to sing. Let me move in closer.

◆ Jamaican singer sings "The First Noel." Singer asks audience to join in on chorus.

◆ Sounds of crowd moving begin. All cast exits the stage slowly, except Magi and Jacob.

◆ Elizabeth remains at her desk.

JACOB: Wow, they are wound up. Let me see if I can interview a few of these people.

◆ Turning to the three Magi who have passed by Jacob

Your highnesses, are you three following the star?

◆ Jacob moves microphone to Magi Mike's mouth, and then to each speaker's mouth throughout the report.

MAGI MIKE: Most definitely.

MAGI MELISSA: Affirmative.

MAGI MARK: Yes. We are. We've been following this star of wonder for several days.

JACOB: And where have you come from?

MAGI MARK: From the far east.

JACOB: So, you're the three kings from the orient.

◆ Magi step forward.

JACOB: ◆ Turns to audience
Join us, please.

◆ Cast and congregation sing "We Three Kings."

◆ The three kings march in place with arms linked together during the verse.

◆ On the refrain "Oh-h-h" they bend their knees, then stand back up.

◆ Alternating lines of the refrain, they look right with right hands over their eyes, then left with left hands over their eyes, then right, then left.

JACOB: ◆ In awe, responding to the last line in the song.
The perfect light? The light from the star, right. And, what do you expect to find there? Gold?

MAGI MIKE: Definitely not.

MAGI MELISSA: Negative. Something much more valuable.

MAGI MARK: Something that's value cannot be measured!

JACOB: But, Magi, what could possibly be so valuable?

ALL THREE: A baby.

JACOB: There you have it, Obadiah, a baby...

◆ **Jacob does a double take.**

...a baby!

◆ **The Magi leave.**

OBADIAH: Thanks, Jacob. We're looking forward to hearing more from you as that story develops. Elizabeth.

ELIZABETH: We'll be right back after this break.

◆ **News theme begins. Commercial announcer enters from stage left and stands center stage.**

COMMERCIAL ANNOUNCER: You need help. You're a fisherman and your net has a hole in it. Why watch profits swim away when help is as close as the tip of your oar. At Net Menders we can repair any size rip while you wait. Whether it was made by a microscopic minnow or a titanic tuna, at Net Menders we'll have you back on the water in just about an hour. And, every Net Menders repair is guaranteed not to rip or tear for 12 months or 12,000 fish, whichever comes first. So whether you're fishing the Mediterranean, Lake Galilee or the Jordan river, remember, there's a Net Menders near you.

◆ **Commercial Announcer exits stage.**

◆ As music plays, Irene and Sam, the shepherd, enter from stage left.

◆ They talk to each other while they stand center stage.

ELIZABETH: For our closing story, we take you to the hills outside Bethlehem where some shepherds have a wild story to tell. We go now to our reporter on the scene, Irene.

IRENE: ◆ Bundled up—she looks cold and windblown.

◆ Not paying attention to Elizabeth, she is speaking over her shoulder to Sam, the shepherd.

You're kidding! You saw how many angels?

◆ Irene notices she's on the air.

Oh, sorry.

◆ Irene holds microphone at her mouth.

Irene on the scene here. I have heard the most remarkable things from Sam, the shepherd. Sam, tell our viewers about it.

◆ Irene moves microphone to Sam's mouth.

SAM: Well, my buddies and I were just mindin' our own business, countin' the sheep, when, when the sky opened and—well, you, you're not going to believe this—but, but angels appeared and spoke to us from on high!

◆ Other shepherds enter from stage right.

◆ Turn towards audience

Why don't you all join us?

◆ Congregation and cast sing "Angels We Have Heard on High."

◆ Shepherds may use the following choreography during the song:

While singing, "Angels we have heard on high, sweetly singing o'er the plains," half the shepherds move their arms in an arch over their heads.

While singing, "And the mountains in reply, echoing their joyous strains," the other shepherds move their arms in an arch over their heads.

At "Gloria..." shepherds grab hands and form a circle, then move in toward the center, move back out and repeat.

On the last "in excelsis deo" shepherds kneel, fold hands and look heavenward.

IRENE: ◆ Holds microphone at mouth
Do you remember what these angels said?
◆ Irene holds microphone at Sam's mouth.

SAM: I'll never forget it. They said, "Give glory to God in heaven, and on earth, let there be peace among the people who please God."

IRENE: ◆ Wide-eyed and leaning toward Sam in awe
Wow.
◆ Suddenly, professional again, Irene holds microphone at her mouth.
Elizabeth, back to you.

◆ Music begins. Jacob enters stage right and stands a short distance from the manger.

◆ The Bethlehem Star enters stage right and shines flashlight over manger.

◆ Shepherds go over and kneel by the manger.

◆ The Magi enter stage right and kneel by the manger.

◆ Mary and Joseph enter stage right and stand by either side of the manger.

ELIZABETH: We've just received word that Jacob has found the spot where the star is shining. We go to Jacob now for a special report.

JACOB: ◆ **Crouching and whispering into his microphone.**
Yes, Elizabeth, I'm a short distance away from a small manger here on one of the back streets of Bethlehem. I don't know if you can see it or not back at the studio, but the star is shining directly over this lowly stable.

ELIZABETH: And what's so special about the manger? Can you tell us more?

JACOB: Let me go in for a closer look.

◆ **Jacob advances, struggles to look over everyone's shoulders and peers closely.**
Why...it is a baby...

◆ **Jacob does a double take.**
...a baby!!

SAM: ◆ **Holds his finger to his lips and turns to Jacob**
Shhh. The child is sleepin'.

MAGI MELISSA: Yes. The little Messiah must not be disturbed.

JACOB AND ELIZABETH: The little Messiah?

MAGI MELISSA: Yes. He is our Savior. Our King. The Messiah... God's son.

MAGI MARK: He will truly bring us closer to God.

◆ **Cast nods in agreement.**

SEVERAL CAST MEMBERS: Hmm. Yes.

MAGI MIKE: And the night is so quiet now. It's... calm and holy. It's truly a silent night.
◆ **Turns to audience**
Join with us, please.

◆ **Congregation and cast sing "Silent Night."**

SAM: Wha... what am I standin' around here for? Everyone needs to hear 'bout this.

◆ **Turns to the audience.**

Will all of you help me go tell it on the mountains and everywhere? Come on, stand up and sing.

◆ **Congregation and cast stand and sing "Go Tell It On the Mountain."**

◆ **Sam and the shepherds run off.**

JACOB: Well, that's the story from the stable, Elizabeth. Although I don't think the story ends here.

ELIZABETH: I think you're right, Jacob. I think you're right. In this reporter's opinion, it looks like the beginning of a far greater story. Well, thank you for tuning in to our special report. From all of us here at the Bethlehem Broadcasting System, we join you—and all of heaven—in celebrating God's gift to us. We close this special broadcast with a look at all the people who brought you this report.

◆ **Music theme begins. Cast assembles on stage.**

ELIZABETH: Join us all in singing "Joy to the World."

◆ **Congregation and cast sing "Joy to the World."**
◆ **As "Joy to the World" is sung, Joseph, Mary and baby Jesus proceed to center stage.**

◆ All participants form a semicircle around them, kneel with hands folded and look at the holy family.

EXIT MUSIC *(Plays as characters and audience exit)*

THE END

O Little Town of Bethlehem

O little town of Bethlehem,
How still we see thee lie!
Above thy deep and dreamless sleep
The silent stars go by.
Yet in the dark streets shineth
The everlasting Light;
The hopes and fears of all the years
Are met in thee tonight.

O holy Child of Bethlehem,
Descend to us, we pray!
Cast out our sin, and enter in,
Be born in us today.
We hear the Christmas angels
The great glad tidings tell;
O come to us, abide with us,
Our Lord Emmanuel!

Away in a Manger

Away in a manger, no crib for a bed,
The little Lord Jesus laid down His sweet head.
The stars in the sky looked down where He lay,
The little Lord Jesus asleep on the hay.

The cattle are lowing, the poor Baby wakes,
But little Lord Jesus, no crying He makes.
I love Thee, Lord Jesus; look down from the sky,
And stay by my cradle till morning is nigh.

We Three Kings

We three kings of Orient are;
Bearing gifts we traverse afar
Field and fountain, moor and mountain
Following yonder star.

O star of wonder, star of night,
Star with royal beauty bright,
Westward leading, still proceeding,
Guide us to thy perfect light.

Glorious now behold Him arise,
King and God and sacrifice,
"Alleluia, Alleluia,"
Earth to the heav'ns replies.

O star of wonder, star of night,
Star with royal beauty bright,
Westward leading, still proceeding,
Guide us to thy perfect light.

Angels We Have Heard on High

Angels we have heard on high,
Sweetly singing o'er the plains;
And the mountains in reply
Echoing their joyous strains.

Shepherds, why this jubilee?
Why your joyous strains prolong?
Say, what may the tidings be;
Which inspired your heav'nly song?

Glo------ria in excelsis Deo!
Glo------ria in excelsis Deo!

Silent Night

Silent night! Holy night!
All is calm, all is bright.
Round yon Virgin Mother and Child!
Holy Infant so tender and mild,
Sleep in heavenly peace,
Sleep in heavenly peace.

Silent night! Holy night!
Darkness flees, all is light;
Shepherds hear the angels sing,
"Alleluia! Hail the King!
Christ, the Savior, is born!
Christ, the Savior, is born!"

Silent night! Holy night!
Son of God, love's our light;
Radiant beams from Thy holy face,
With the dawn of redeeming grace,
Jesus, Lord at Thy birth.
Jesus, Lord at Thy birth.

Go Tell It on the Mountain

(chorus)
Go, tell it on the mountain,
Over the hills and everywhere;
Go, tell it on the mountain,
That Jesus Christ is born!

Down in a lowly manger
The humble Christ was born,
And brought us God's salvation
That blessed Christmas morn.
(chorus)

While shepherds kept their watching
O'er silent flocks by night,
Behold throughout the heavens
There shone a holy light
(Repeat chorus twice)

Joy to the World

Joy to the world! The Lord is come;
Let earth receive her King;
Let ev'ry heart prepare Him room
And heav'n and nature sing,
And heav'n and nature sing,
And heav'n and heav'n and nature sing.

Joy to the world! the Savior reigns;
Let men their songs employ,
While fields and floods, rocks, hills,
 and plains,
Repeat the sounding joy,
Repeat the sounding joy,
Repeat, repeat the sounding joy.

No more let sin and sorrow grow,
Nor thorns infest the ground;
He comes to make His blessings flow
Far as the curse is found,
Far as the curse is found,
Far as, far as the curse is found.

Permission to photocopy this lyric sheet from *Instant Christmas Pageant: Live from Bethlehem* granted for local church use.
Copyright © Group Publishing, Inc., Box 481, Loveland, CO 80539.

More Resources for Your Children's Ministry

Quick Children's Sermons: Will My Dog Be in Heaven?

Kids ask the most amazing questions—and now you'll be ready to answer 50 of them! You'll get witty, wise, and biblically solid answers to kid-size questions...and each question and answer makes a wonderful children's sermon. This is an attention-grabbing resource for children's pastors, Sunday school teachers, church workers, and parents.

ISBN 1-55945-612-4

"Let's Play!" Group Games for Preschoolers

Make playtime learning time with great games that work in any size class! Here are more than 140 easy-to-lead, fun-to-play games that teach preschoolers about Bible characters and stories. You'll love the clear, simple directions, and your kids will love that they can actually do these games!

ISBN 1-55945-613-2

More Than Mud Pies

Preschoolers love making crafts...but finished crafts are often forgotten long before the glue dries. Until now! These 48 3-D crafts become fun games your preschoolers will play again and again. And every time they play, your preschoolers will be reminded of important Bible truths. Each craft comes with photocopiable game instructions to send home to parents!

ISBN 0-7644-2044-5

The Discipline Guide for Children's Ministry

Jody Capehart, Gordon West & Becki West

With this book you'll understand and implement classroom-management techniques that work—and that make teaching fun again! From a thorough explanation of age-appropriate concerns...to proven strategies for heading off discipline problems before they occur...here's a practical book you'll turn to again and again!

ISBN 1-55945-686-8

Order today from your local Christian bookstore, or write: Group Publishing, P.O. Box 485, Loveland, CO 80539.